# An Introduction to Information Security and

# ISO27001:2013

## A Pocket Guide

Second edition

# An Introduction to Information Security and ISO27001:2013

## A Pocket Guide

### Second edition

STEVE G WATKINS

**IT Governance Publishing**

Every possible effort has been made to ensure that the information contained in this book is accurate at the time of going to press, and the publisher and the author cannot accept responsibility for any errors or omissions, however caused. Any opinions expressed in this book are those of the author, not the publisher. Websites identified are for reference only, not endorsement, and any website visits are at the reader's own risk. No responsibility for loss or damage occasioned to any person acting, or refraining from action, as a result of the material in this publication can be accepted by the publisher or the author.

Apart from any fair dealing for the purposes of research or private study, or criticism or review, as permitted under the Copyright, Designs and Patents Act 1988, this publication may only be reproduced, stored or transmitted, in any form, or by any means, with the prior permission in writing of the publisher or, in the case of reprographic reproduction, in accordance with the terms of licences issued by the Copyright Licensing Agency. Enquiries concerning reproduction outside those terms should be sent to the publisher at the following address:

IT Governance Publishing
IT Governance Limited
Unit 3, Clive Court, Bartholomew's Walk
Cambridgeshire Business Park
Ely, Cambridgeshire
CB7 4EA
United Kingdom

www.itgovernance.co.uk

First published in the United Kingdom in 2008
by IT Governance Publishing.

Second edition published in 2013.

ISBN 978-1-84928-526-1

# ABOUT THE AUTHOR

Steve G Watkins: Director, Training and Consultancy, IT Governance Ltd.

Steve managed the world's first successful BS7799 (the forerunner of ISO27001) implementation project; he leads the consultancy and training services of IT Governance.

He is Chair of the ISO/IEC 27001 User Group, the UK Chapter of the ISMS International User Group, and an ISMS Technical Assessor for UKAS, advising on their assessments of certification bodies offering accredited certification.

Steve sits on the IST/33 committee responsible for the UK's contributions to the revisions of the ISO 2700x series of standards and RM/1, the committee responsible for BS31100/ISO31000, the British Standard for Risk Management and the UK's contributions to ISO31000. Steve is also co-author (with Alan Calder) of the definitive compliance guide, *IT Governance: An International Guide to Data Security and ISO 27001/ISO27002*.

He has over 20 years' experience of managing integrated management systems, including maintenance of Information Security, Quality, Environmental and Investor in People certifications. His experience includes senior management positions in both the public and private sector.

Steve regularly tweets information security and privacy matters using *@swatty70*. He can be contacted at:

*swatkins@itgovernance.co.uk*.

# CONTENTS

# INTRODUCTION

This pocket guide is intended to meet the needs of two groups:

1. Individual readers who have turned to it as an introduction to a topic that they know little about.
2. Organisations implementing, or considering implementing, some sort of information security management regime, particularly if using ISO/IEC 27001:2013, who wish to raise awareness.

In either case the guide furnishes readers with an understanding of the basics of information security, including:

- A definition of what information security means.
- How managing information security can be achieved using an approach recognised worldwide.
- The factors that need to be considered in an information security regime, including how the perimeters of such a scheme can be properly defined.
- How an information security management system can ensure it is maximising the effect of any budget it has.
- Key areas of investment for a business-focused information security management system.
- How organisations can demonstrate the degree of assurance they offer with regard to information security, how to interpret claims of adherence to the ISO27001 Standard and exactly what that means.

Corporate bodies will find this guide useful at a number of stages in any information security project, including:

- At the decision-making stage, to ensure that those committing to an information security project do so from an informed position.
- At project initiation, as an introduction to information security for the project board, project team members and those on the periphery of the project.

- As part of an ongoing awareness campaign, being made available to all staff[1] and to new starters as part of their introduction to the company.

Corporate users may find they get the most benefit by making this pocket guide available and adding a small flyer inside it, which explains how various sections relate to their own specific environment, or where the issues raised in this guide are addressed in their own Information Security Management System (ISMS). For example:

> A Real
> Co Ltd
>
> **When things go wrong: (Chapter 5)**
>
> When you witness a security incident you are required to report it in accordance with DOC 16.1, Reporting Information Security Events procedure.

This pocket guide is designed to be read without having to break frequently from the text, but there is a list of abbreviations along with terms and definitions in *Chapter 7* for easy reference. Where footnotes have been added they are not essential reading, and it is recommended you ignore these on your first read through if you are new to the subject – on a second reading they will be of more relevance, and particularly

---

[1] Why not conduct sample surveys of people's understanding of some aspects of information security and compile the results both before and after the start of your awareness campaign to demonstrate the effectiveness of your communications and use the figures as one of your effectiveness measures and feed this into management review? See ISO27001:2013 sections 7.2, 9.1.a and 9.3.c.2.

if you are involved in an information security project or decision at any stage.

A word of warning: this is not an implementation or 'How to do it' guide.

Implementing an ISO27001-compliant ISMS requires more advice than a pocket guide such as this could possibly offer. The project is in most cases likely to equate to a significant business-change project, and will require all the project governance arrangements that suit such an undertaking.

There are books available which offer suitably detailed advice, such as *IT Governance: A Manager's Guide to Data Security and ISO 27001/ ISO27002* (5th edition) and they can be obtained along with numerous other helpful advice, tools and other related information from the sources signposted in *Chapter 7*.

# CHAPTER 1: INFORMATION SECURITY – WHAT'S THAT?

To develop an understanding of what information security means, let's consider something that we all understand the value of: money.

Considering the various aspects of how you look after and use your money, the following emerge as valuable and worthy of note:

## Aspect One

*You do not want other people spending your money, or at least anyone not given your permission to spend it. This means limiting access to your money, or, when considering information instead of money, keeping it confidential.*

This makes good sense, and at first pass may seem to be the only thing that matters. However, if restricting access to your money is all that matters you could have it stored in a totally sealed iron box. Not very useful when you come to want to spend it yourself! This brings us on to our second aspect:

## Aspect Two

*You want to be able to spend your money when you want to. This means you value the availability of it. Not only this, but you need it to be available in a usable format and timely manner, so if you are abroad you want the money to be in the correct currency when you come to spend it.*

This also makes good sense. We have identified that in controlling our money we need to consider both restricting access to it (an appropriate degree of confidentiality) and ensuring this is balanced with a suitable degree of availability. However, there is another value that we should be concerned with, and to explain this we might consider the issue of foreign currency a little further.

## Aspect Three

*When collecting your currency, you do not — at least when first visiting a part of the world that is new to you — know what the money should look like or how you can be assured it is not fake. Most people are content to rely on the reputation of whatever company they choose to exchange their cash with. Nonetheless, we do value the fact that what we are being provided with is the real thing and not counterfeit. This is to say that we value the integrity of what we receive.*

So with money we value keeping it out of the hands of others, having it accessible when we want it and in the format that we want it in, and that it is what it appears to be. When related to information integrity this can be summarised as 'complete and accurate'.

When referring to information this is the equivalent of valuing the information's confidentiality, availability and integrity; hence, when managing the security of information we need to consider these three aspects – much more than the layman's understanding of the word 'security'!

Organisations that wish to manage their information security arrangements typically introduce a set of policies, processes and working arrangements that help them exercise a degree of control to provide assurance with regard to these three aspects. This is generically described as an Information Security Management System (ISMS).

## Who does it matter to?

Given the definition of information security as the preservation of the confidentiality, integrity and availability of information,[1] it is relatively easy to determine why this might be of importance to individuals, companies and public bodies.

---

[1] ISO/IEC 27000:2012 defines information security as the 'preservation of confidentiality, integrity and availability of information; in addition, other properties such as authenticity, accountability, non-repudiation and reliability can also be involved'.

It soon becomes obvious that it is not just the information that we need to be concerned with, but the storage, handling, moving and processing of it. When considering all of these arrangements it is relatively easy to conclude that every organisation should be concerned with their information security arrangements.

Individuals (members of the public or customers and staff) will want to know that information held about them is being managed and protected appropriately. Theft or fraud involving credit cards, credit ratings and people's very identities are well-publicised issues that mean information security is worthy of attention.

Companies will be driven by at least two factors: the requirements of their stakeholders and/or customers, and the need to remain competitive, protecting their IPR and reputation. Public-sector organisations have similar drivers to maintain a strong security stance and safeguard against security incidents.

In fact, many sectors have regulators that demand some suitable form of information management to be in place for anyone offering related services. Various governance regimes include requirements for information and information-processing arrangements, demanding that there are controls in place to enable directors to discharge their duties effectively. With high-profile governance failures in the headlines this is an area where pressure to comply will only grow.[2]

With the increasing trend towards relying on business partners for key services and processes, the need for some form of information security assurance is well recognised. Outsourcing and other contracts are now increasingly specifying compliance with some form of information governance regime as a mandatory requirement.[3]

---

[2] See *IT Governance: Guidelines for Directors* by Alan Calder for further information, available through *www.itgovernance.co.uk*.
[3] More on what assurances such schemes provide and on how to interpret any claims is provided in *Chapter 6*.

The other key driver is the need to maintain a competitive edge. The obvious aims of not informing competitors of your costs, customers or trade secrets are concerns that fall within the remit of information security management, as are the less obvious benefits of effective information security such as improvements in customer service through appropriately managed databases (e.g. no longer sending mail shots to addresses that the client has told you they have moved from).

An effective information security management regime can provide an organisation with the foundations on which to build a knowledge management strategy and realise the true value of all the information that it holds.

The public sector has its own drivers, of course, including issues such as justice and national security, as well as the responsibility to become as effective and efficient as possible in conducting its work, in order to be able to truly demonstrate appropriate stewardship of public funds.

To all this should be added the obvious requirement that staff from any organisation will expect their personal information to be managed appropriately and their right to privacy respected.

## CHAPTER 2: IT'S NOT IT

The key message in this chapter is that an effective Information Security Management System (ISMS) needs to address issues relating to personnel, facilities, suppliers and cultural issues, in addition to the obvious area of information technology, and so information security is a topic that goes well beyond the remit of IT, whether that be the equipment, department or service[1].

Having identified what information security is, and recognising it as something worth being concerned about, the next stage is to determine exactly what areas and aspects of the organisation will be affected.

Starting with the source of the challenge, we need to consider the 'external and internal issues' that are likely to affect our business, 'interested parties' (e.g. regulators and clients) and information security requirements of these parties to ensure that the ISMS is relevant to our organisation and provides an assurance that is appropriate to our stakeholders. It is then a case of including everything that can affect our information, which means including all the equipment on which that information is held, how it is moved/transmitted and any aspects of the business that can affect the information, equipment and related processes. This means we need to set both physical and logical perimeters for our ISMS.

In practice this means that it is necessary to consider the dependencies and interfaces of all aspects of the management system and the information it controls. For example, if we consider information that is sent by courier to another office of the same organisation then we need to include the selection of

---

[1] Cyber security, a discipline closely related to information security, is defined as encompassing the protection of all electronically facilitated business information and processes, and all information and control systems. As such, it encompasses the fields of information assurance and information security across technical, people and physical domains (PAS 555:2012).

the courier company and the security requirements placed on the courier through the contract.

With regard to confidentiality it is necessary to consider everyone who has access to the information and the equipment on which it is stored. This is likely to include cleaners and maintenance staff, in addition to directly employed staff.

The system also needs to address the management of information in different formats, including electronic form and hardcopy documents. With information in transit — whether it be in the form of papers being taken home for reviewing the night prior to a meeting, or records being sent to archive — it becomes obvious that hardcopy documents warrant a similar degree of protection to electronic copies. If a trade secret is accessed by a competitor it does not matter whether it is in an e-mail attachment or printed on a piece of paper: the information that was meant to be kept confidential is in the hands of, or available via a means that results in unauthorised access and so any value attached to maintaining its confidentiality is compromised. The value of information is in its content, not in the format it is stored or available in.

Considering these issues, one way or another the ISMS needs to define how it addresses relationships with suppliers, business partners, customers and staff. Of course, the facilities and equipment used to protect and provide information are of equal importance, and also need to be considered within the scope of the ISMS.

In defining the remit of the ISMS this way the organisation is stating the scope of the assurance the system provides. Given the personnel, facilities, suppliers and cultural issues that need to be considered and addressed within the system, it is obviously a topic that goes well beyond the remit of the IT department.

# CHAPTER 3: ISO27001 AND THE MANAGEMENT SYSTEM REQUIREMENTS

As with most topics, there are international standards that deal with information security management, and the main one is ISO27001:2013.[1]

This Standard is structured in a linear fashion, from the establishment of the ISMS through to the review and adaptation of the ISMS. However, addressing the requirements in that order is not a requirement in itself. In the previous edition, the Standard defined the project approach as the well-recognised Plan–Do–Check–Act model (P-D-C-A) to structure the tasks required to introduce an effective ISMS. While this is no longer strictly mandated by ISO27001, it remains a valid and effective approach.

The P-D-C-A cycle can be summarised as:

- Plan what you need to do to achieve the objective (which includes defining what that objective is).
- Do what you planned.
- Check that what you have done achieves what you had planned for it to achieve and identify any gaps or shortfalls (i.e. check whether you have met the objectives).
- Act on the findings of the check phase to address the gaps and/or improve the efficiency and effectiveness of what you have in place.

Typically this last stage will involve making a plan, doing what that plan entails, checking that the objectives were achieved,

---

[1] Other standards that have been used in referencing information security management over a number of years include BS7799 and ISO17799, but ISO27001 is now the Standard for the specification of an Information Security Management System. ISO27002 provides guidance on the implementation of information security controls catalogued at Annex A of ISO27001.

identifying any shortfalls and then acting on the findings by once again creating a plan.

And so, with the introduction of an ISMS using P-D-C-A, the initial cycle of continuous improvement is effected.

One common misunderstanding in adopting the P-D-C-A approach is that the planning stage is limited purely to planning the project. However, applying the approach required in the 2005 version of ISO27001, the planning stage includes all the activity to determine what is required of the ISMS, and how this is to be achieved. This is a significant undertaking, to the extent that it can take up to half of the project time from initiation through to having a full ISMS in place. The other main resource-demanding stage is implementation. The next chapter deals with the most resource-intensive aspects of determining what is required of the ISMS.

There are a number of requirements for a management system to operate that are as applicable to an ISMS as to any other management system, and these include:

- **Document control.** This is an arrangement to manage the availability of documents within the ISMS, typically including:

    - the corporate-level policies
    - operating procedures which describe the processes that support the policy and explain who does what, where and when
    - work instructions that detail how certain tasks should be conducted, and
    - records which capture the information that is essential for the purposes of review and to inform decisions. These include documents such as audit schedules and logs, records of work completed for the purpose of traceability and accountability, etc.

The aim of document control is to ensure that all these documents have been written and approved by the right people and that only the latest approved versions are available to those who need to be aware of and follow them. Records also need to be safeguarded once they are generated. This means protecting their confidentiality, integrity and availability in order to be sure they can be retrieved by the right (authorised) people when needed and that they are legible and have not been interfered with.

Returning to the common management system 'hygiene' factors …

- **Internal audit.** Internal audits can be used for many purposes, but one of the main objectives of deploying an internal management system audit programme is to monitor compliance between the management system requirements and working practice. The internal audits are commissioned by the organisation, for the organisation, and provide an opportunity to review the level of compliance within and effectiveness of the ISMS. This is achieved by examining what actually happens across a sample of activities and processes and comparing this to what the documented management system describes. The identification of any mismatch during an audit provides the opportunity to put it right, either by changing the system description of what happens, by enhancing working practices, or addressing competency issues (often through improved training and awareness). The internal audit process should also inform the continual improvement of the ISMS; however, this typically only starts to become an objective of audits once the ISMS is embedded. Internal audits can also be commissioned to target specific areas of concern or for the purpose of identifying opportunities for improvement.
- **Management review.** Given that management initiate the ISMS by approving the use of resources to undertake the project and issuing the corporate information security policy defining the objectives of the ISMS, it is reasonable to expect them to review the progress of the implementation project and the effectiveness of the ISMS

thereafter. The management review is typically held once every six or 12 months and is intended to achieve exactly these objectives. A number of reports would be prepared for the meeting, covering key indicators of how the ISMS is operating. These reports include an analysis of the outcome of audits (internal and second- and third-party[2]), significant security-related incidents, changes in external and internal issues that may affect the ISMS, some form of indicator of awareness of information security issues and the ISMS across all those affected by it, and an indication of the amount and timeliness of any improvement activity undertaken. The review should also examine the effectiveness measures[3] that have been developed and any opportunities for continual improvement that have been identified or implemented.

---

[2] See *Chapter 6* for further information on second- and third-party audits.

[3] ISO27001:2013 requires the organisation to define how the effectiveness of the information security management system will be measured (including at sections 5.1 d, 6.1.1.e.2, 7.2 c, 9.1 and in particular 9.1.b) and for the management to consider them (section 9.3.c.2).

# CHAPTER 4: LEGAL, REGULATORY AND CONTRACTUAL REQUIREMENTS AND BUSINESS RISK

The specific security requirements of an ISMS are determined in light of the purpose of the organisation and its objectives. To achieve this it is required that those with an interest in the performance of the organisation, and their information security specific requirements are identified. These requirements, together with the specific legal, regulatory and contractual obligations on the organisation form the starting point of the ISMS security arrangements, and these are combined with the results of an information security risk assessment to determine the blend of security controls on which the organisation will rely.

ISO27001 does not dictate a particular methodology and there are many to choose from. What follows here is a general description of a risk assessment you might expect to see in an effective ISMS.

To undertake the risk assessment it is necessary to have defined the scope of the ISMS.

For the risk assessment to be effective it is necessary to consider everything that might go wrong with respect to information – this will need to include information, information processing and storage equipment (every server, computer, laptop, PDA, mobile phone), systems, staff, buildings, etc.[1].

Risks need to be identified and estimated for the three information security attributes: confidentiality, integrity and availability in a manner whereby the results are comparable and reproducible. The 'consequence' assigned to each risk

---

[1] Advice on information security risk assessment is more complex than can be covered in this pocket guide. See *Information Security Risk Management for ISO 27001/ ISO27002* by Alan Calder and Steve G Watkins for more information.

reflects the total cost to the organisation if that risk was to materialise, from the cost of replacement, through the consequences for the process(es) it is involved in, to the impact on the organisation's reputation. This is normally best estimated by those involved in the relevant business processes.

These values provide the impact aspect of the classic

$$\text{Risk}^2 = \text{Likelihood} \times \text{Impact}$$

relationship.

The risk assessment then uses these estimates, and those of the likelihood of the risk coming to fruition, to determine the risk values. The relationship between likelihood, impact and risk is demonstrated in the following diagram, in this case showing three levels of likelihood and three levels of impact, which together give five levels of risk varying from 'very low' through to 'very high':

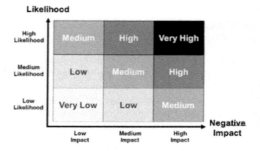

---

[2] ISO27000:2012 defines risk as 'the effectiveness of uncertainty on objectives' and goes on to stage in a note that information security risk is often expressed in terms of a combination of the consequences of an information security event and the associated likelihood of occurrence.

The main aim of an ISMS is to manage all risks to a consistent level, and management need to determine what level of risk is acceptable. For example, they may, using the parameters in the diagram above, decide that risks up to and including 'low' are acceptable, and that therefore it is only those risks that have been assessed as falling above that level of 'risk acceptance criteria' that need managing. In terms of the diagram, the risk acceptance level can be demonstrated by the shaded area as shown here:

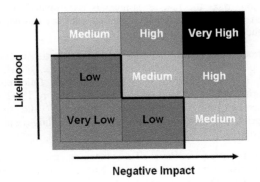

**Negative Impact**

Each organisation will have a different level of risk acceptance and this will relate to the organisation's risk appetite – the degree of risk that the organisation is happy to live with on a day-to-day basis. Each risk is assigned to a risk owner, who will be responsible for approving the risk treatment and accepting any residual risk, in light of the risk acceptance criteria.

Risks assessed as falling above the acceptable level are considered and a decision taken as to what to do about each of them. This decision determines which one or more of the following options to apply to address the identified risk:

1. Apply controls to reduce the risk. (Treat)

2.  Accept the risk; this is normally determined by the risk acceptance criteria, but can occasionally be applied even if the risk level is above the acceptable level. (Tolerate)

3.  Avoid the risk by identifying a work-around that negates the risk. (Terminate)

4.  Transfer the business risk to an insurer or supplier. (Transfer – accommodated in the control set at Annex A of the Standard)

As different decisions and controls are selected for application to various risks the risk assessment is re-estimated and this process continues until all the assessed risks are estimated to meet the risk acceptance criteria.

The process of determining controls to manage risk is critical to the performance of the ISMS. In the first stage, you should design a set of controls to manage the risk, followed by comparing this list of controls to those at Annex A. ISO27001 controls can and should be taken from any valid source appropriate to the organisation or process, including designing them yourself.

To effect the required level of assurance against information security risks, the ISMS needs to ensure that the controls identified as necessary to meet legal, regulatory and contractual obligations and selected through the risk assessment process are in place and applied effectively. By informing the selection of information security controls with this approach an organisation can ensure that it is maximising the effectiveness of its information security spend, and not leaving any one area of risk open to exploitation at the cost of an inconsistently high level of control elsewhere.

ISO27001 requires a document to be produced that details which controls are applied within the ISMS and which are not. This is known as the 'Statement of Applicability' (SoA).

The process to determine the right blend of security controls within the ISMS requires a degree of central coordination, and often benefits from the use of a suitable software solution that can automate many of the potentially resource-intensive administration aspects of the process. The investment in such software really pays back when the ISMS gets into continuous improvement, as the risk assessment needs to be revisited, either in part or as a whole.

# CHAPTER 5: INFORMATION SECURITY CONTROLS

Having now gained an appreciation of the methodical approach to the selection of information security controls and other ways of addressing risks, it is time to examine the security controls defined in the international ISMS Standards.

The Standards themselves emphasise that the controls they detail are to be used to ensure that none have been inappropriately omitted and that they are not a default control set to build upon. Typically an organisation would start with sector and contract specific requirements and then consider others. There will also be technological developments that introduce risks which are not covered to a suitable extent by the security controls listed at Annex A, and so it may be necessary to adopt further controls.

In ISO27001 there are 114 controls split into 14 categories, but for the purpose of familiarisation here we are considering them in six groups, and not in any detail. The six groups are not themselves significant and they could easily be formed differently.

## Information security organisation, structure and human resources

This list includes the main controls off which the rest of the system hangs. There is a need for a corporate-level information security policy, which is a statement of the organisation's commitment and objectives relating to information security and then others that support and deliver the intent of this. The highest-level policy needs to be available to everyone affected by it, which (as described earlier) includes suppliers, business partners, customers and staff.

There is a need to define where responsibilities for information security lie within the organisation and for the required forums and review bodies to be in place to meet the needs of the ISMS. A similar set of requirements are implied in the control category relating to supplier relationships, with the need to agree respective roles, responsibilities, actions and liabilities.

The human resources required to undertake all tasks relating to and affecting information security need to be sourced and managed appropriately. This includes considering the sourcing, vetting, management and exiting arrangements for staff, contractors and any other people who interact with the scope of the ISMS, including anyone who has physical access to any premises at or from which information-related assets can be accessed.

## Assets, classification and access control

The asset register needs to go beyond the classic fixed-asset register and include information assets.

There is a control suggesting that assets are classified to a defined labelling scheme, and the classification will indicate the level of protection required and who has approved access rights to them. Access control is also related to ensuring that only those with approved access to the assets can actually access them, and this is subject to both logical and/or physical barriers.

Passwords and user IT accounts are typical logical access controls, and are of course only as robust as the practices that manage them. Eradicating poor practices such as writing passwords down, or using sequential or easily guessable combinations, should be strongly discouraged.

Where access issues are risk assessed as requiring a greater degree of assurance — with regard to accessing a system or application remotely, for example — there is the possibility of two-factor authentication. This is where each unique user has to deploy, in combination, two out of the three factors — physical key (token), a logical key (password) and/or a personal attribute (retina scan, voice verification or finger print scan) — to be granted access. An example is a debit card being used to withdraw cash from an ATM (the magnetic strip or smart chip being the physical key) and your personal identification number (PIN – the logical key). Of course, when using a payment card online the physical aspect normally disappears if you have sufficient details to hand in another format, and hence the request for further numbers which are normally sourced from the card, or passwords separate from your PIN. Some banks address this weakness by issuing card readers to account holders and asking that they use these for authentication of the person triggering the transaction and particularly for online banking.

With continuing advances in technology it is increasingly challenging to remain ahead of thieves and crackers or hackers. Passwords can often be broken and whilst encryption (the use of pairs of numeric algorithms, or keys, one to scramble information and its counterpart to unscramble it) provides an enhanced level of unwanted access prevention (logical, not physical), there are incidents of encryption controls being beaten, most often due to the mismanagement of keys, and so the combination of logical and physical controls is essential to an efficient, effective ISMS.

There are also controls which can be deployed, such as session timeouts, that require the user to re-enter selected logon criteria every so often and duress alarms that consist of a predetermined series of apparently innocuous key strokes which alert network or system monitors to a problem without making anyone in the vicinity of the user aware that an alarm has been activated.

### Physical access and environmental issues

Physical access is, of course, a concern for information security. Anyone who has access to the equipment or medium on which information is stored could potentially walk out with that asset and the information assets stored on it. Whilst some protection can be offered to prevent access to information stolen in this manner, it will still affect the availability of that information and possibly the resulting integrity of the data asset as well.

Perimeters around secure areas should be defined in all three dimensions – tunnelling in through the floor, or using an air vent in the ceiling, may still allow enough access and egress for theft to take place.

There are also controls relating to the dependency on utilities and the environment – power cuts and adverse weather conditions provide regular tests of security arrangements and their ability to make sure the systems and information on which the business relies continue to be available.

## Networks and IT

The largest number of controls relate to IT operations and network management. They cover issues including planning and testing new developments prior to implementation, capacity planning for all aspects of the network and systems, segregation, network design and technical vulnerability management. Issues such as back-up are mentioned here, which includes testing of the back-up so that, as an example, any accidentally deleted filed can be restored from the copy of all files (the back-up) run the previous night.

## When things go wrong

There are a number of categories which deal with the handling of problems, events and/or incidents.[1] These are additional to the improvement-process requirements of maintaining an ISMS, and deal with what should be done in reaction to, and in order to recover from, a security breach.

The severity of information security breaches can vary massively. If the problem is likely to cause a significant challenge to the normal running of operations it is desirable for some form of business continuity to be invoked. This area of

---

[1] ISO27000 defines information security incidents and information security events separately. Not all events are, or will be, incidents, but both require action and this should be defined. Clarification should also be given as to when an event escalates to incident level or be classified as such.

control includes the need to regularly test the business continuity plans (BCPs) in order to learn from the experience and improve the plans ahead of their being called upon for real.

Of course, not all security incidents require such a dramatic response, but the degree of reaction and the method for determining escalation should be defined.

All of these issues are key areas for information security awareness campaigns, as the organisation should be in a position to benefit from notification of a potential problem as soon as possible. This therefore means that awareness needs to be raised and maintained for all relevant parties, including suppliers, business partners, customers and staff. Often cleaners will be among the first people at a site each day, or the last to leave it, and they should be trained and required by contract to report any security-related observations to an appropriate contact.

## Compliance and audit

These categories are relatively self-explanatory: they deal with legal and technical compliance. The organisation should be aware of, and comply with, its legal obligations and contractual requirements. Technical testing should report on the degree to which IT equipment, systems and software are as they should be. The schedule can include checks to confirm that only the right, approved equipment is connected to the network, that systems and software are as required (the approved mix and number for the licences held), and can include penetration testing to confirm the resilience of the technical measures in place.

# CHAPTER 6: CERTIFICATION

As with many other management system standards, there is a scheme that can be used by organisations to demonstrate their compliance with the internationally recognised Standard for information security management, ISO27001.

Companies wishing to use this scheme to demonstrate the robustness of their information security management arrangements need to subject themselves to an external audit.

For the assurance provided by the outcome of the audit to be recognised[1], the audit needs to be conducted in compliance with the recognised scheme; that is, the 'accredited certification scheme'. This is administered by the United Kingdom Accreditation Service (UKAS) in the UK and certificates issued under this scheme will bear the UKAS logo:

The audits are conducted by accredited certification bodies; those seeking to demonstrate compliance with the Standard become certificated, not accredited.

---

[1] Non-accredited certification is available and offers a view from a single audit body's perspective, one that is not subject to the 'check and challenge' of the worldwide accredited certification scheme.

Accreditation bodies around the world sign up to a memorandum of understanding that results in mutual recognition of each other's schemes – so a certificate issued by the ANSI-ASQ National Accreditation Board (ANAB) in America, the Joint Accreditation System of Australia and New Zealand (JAS-ANZ) or another member of the IAF[2] will be the equivalent of one issued by UKAS – hence a worldwide scheme exists.

The scheme enables suppliers to demonstrate a degree of assurance with regard to their information security practices. The integrity of this scheme means that customers can rely on certification rather than insist on sending their own auditors in to provide the assurances required by their own directors, stakeholders and clients[3]. This can save a lot of time, cost and disruption for both the auditing and audited parties – a benefit that contributes to the uptake of ISO27001-accredited certification.

However, claims of ISO27001 certification are often misinterpreted, or used as a guarantee where they should not be.

To gain certification, the organisation needs to comply with ISO27001, which means that it must have a scope defining the extent of its ISMS (or at least the extent of the ISMS that is certificated) and a statement of applicability (SoA) that defines what controls are applied across which aspects of the ISMS.

It is these two documents, together with the accredited certificate, that provide evidence of the level of assurance the organisation's ISMS provides regarding its information security practices.

---

[2] To find out if an accredited certificate is the equivalent of those issued under the scheme described here, determine whether the accreditation body is a member of the International Accreditation Forum (www.iaf.nu).

[3] Some customers may wish to conduct supplier audits as well, in which case ISO27001 certification should provide the framework, terms and definitions as well as a familiarity for that from the outset.

ISO27001 is not a product certification scheme, and to rely on it as such is nonsensical. Accredited certification to ISO27001 provides a service assurance.

## Other audit applications

The provision of a specification for an ISMS lends itself to supplier or second-party audits. This means that buyers can rely on the Standard to provide a recognised and widely available framework against which to conduct supplier audits. These can be used to assure themselves that the level of information security their supplier is providing is in line with the terms of the contract between the two organisations.

Second-party audits can be used by both the auditing and audited parties along similar lines as first-party (see Internal audits in *Chapter 3*) and third-party (see Certification audits in this chapter) audits, benefiting both organisations and driving continuous improvement through the supply chain. However, second party, or supplier audits can prove expensive and are often only used where the degree of risk warrants them. Often the assurance of accredited certification, together with some suitably intelligent questioning is more cost effective.

# CHAPTER 7: SIGNPOSTING

For access to a comprehensive set of all things relating to information security see:

*www.itgovernance.co.uk*.

For general advice that is as applicable to the home as the office take a look at:

*www.getsafeonline.org*.

## Terms

Definitions that have been taken from ISO/IEC 20000-1:2012 are identified thus: *

**Accreditation:** the scheme through which an authoritative body formally recognises a person's or organisation's competence to carry out specified tasks. Not to be confused with certification. Third-party certification (auditing) bodies become accredited and those they audit, subject to a successful outcome, become certificated.

**Asset:** anything that has value to the organisation.* Information assets are likely to be of the following types:

- Information: databases and data files, other files and copies of plans, system documentation, original user manuals, original training material, operational or other support procedures, continuity plans, other fall-back arrangements, archived information, financial and accounting information.
- Business processes: setting your organisation apart from competitors, included in your IPR.
- Software: application software, operating and system software, development tools and utilities, e-learning assets, network tools and utilities.
- Physical: computer equipment (including workstations, notebooks, PDAs, monitors, modems, scanning

machines, printers), communications equipment (routers, mobile phones, PABXs, fax machines, answering machines, voice conferencing units, etc.), magnetic media (tapes and disks), other technical equipment (power supplies, air-conditioning units), furniture, lighting, other equipment.

- Services: 'groups of assets which act together to provide a particular function', such as computing and communications services and general utilities, e.g. heating, lighting, power, air-conditioning.
- People: staff and others have access to, can store and repeat information

**Availability:** property of being accessible and usable upon demand by an authorized entity.*

**Certification:** the process through which a certification body confirms that a product, process or service conforms to a specific standard or specification. For example, an organisation becomes certificated to ISO27001:2013.

**Certification body:** *see* Third-Party certification body.

**Compliance:** a positive answer to the question 'Is what is taking place in line with the pre-specified requirements?' Hence non-compliance and compliance monitoring. Compliance is often used in a legal context.

**Conformance:** fulfilment of a requirement. A positive answer to the question 'Is what is taking place in line with the pre-specified requirements?' Hence non-conformance and conformance monitoring. Conformance is often used in a non-legal context.

**Document control:** a system whereby all documents within the system are managed in a manner to ensure that the currency of the document is always clear. When a controlled document is amended, all copies of it should be simultaneously withdrawn and replaced by the new version.

**Encryption:** the conversion of plain text into code, using a mathematical algorithm, to prevent it being read by a third party.

**Information security event:** an identified occurrence in a system, service or network indicating a possible breach of information security policy or failure of safeguards, or a previously unknown situation that may be security-relevant.* (*See also* Information security incident).

**Information security incident: single or series of** unwanted or unexpected information security events that have a significant probability of compromising business operations and threatening information security.*

**Information security management system (ISMS):** part of the overall management system, based on a business risk approach, to establish, implement, operate, monitor, review, maintain and improve information security.*

**Information security policy:** the organisation's policy for securing its information assets.

**ISMS:** *see* Information security management system.

**ISO:** acronym, from the Greek *isos* ('equal to'), adopted by the International Organisation for Standardisation – the world's largest developer of standards. Its membership comprises the national-standards bodies of countries around the world.

**ISO27002:2013:** the international code of best practice for information security controls which underpins and provides guidance for the implementation of an ISMS, specifically the revised version issued in 2013. It includes individual information security control objectives, security controls, implementation guidance and other information relating to these.

**IT governance:** a framework for standards of leadership, organisational structure and business processes, and for compliance with these standards, which ensures that the organisation's IT supports and enables the achievement of its strategies and objectives.

**Policy:** overall intention and direction as formally expressed by management.*

**Project governance:** the framework and rules controlling how project decisions are made and project activity monitored.

**Registrar:** Americanism for certification body; *see* Certification body.

**Risk:** effect of uncertainty on objectives.*

The definition in ISO27000 goes on to say that risk 'is often characterized by reference to potential events and consequences, or a combination of these' and that 'Information security risk is often expressed in terms of a combination of the consequences of an information security event and the associated likelihood of occurrence'.

**Risk acceptance:** decision to accept a risk.*

**Risk analysis:** process to comprehend the nature of risk and to determine the level of risk.*

**Risk appetite:** an organisation's overall attitude to risk, the balance between risk and return, and the trade-off between security and flexibility, usually a strategic decision by the organisation's board.

**Risk assessment:** overall process of risk identification, risk analysis and risk evaluation.*

**Risk management:** coordinated activities to direct and control an organisation with regard to risk* (usually includes risk assessment, risk treatment, risk acceptance and risk communication).

**SoA:** *see* Statement of Applicability.

**Statement of Applicability (SoA):** documented statement describing the control objectives and controls that are relevant and applicable to the organisation's ISMS, based on the results and conclusions of the risk assessment and risk treatment processes.

**Third-party certification body:** independent organisation with the necessary competence and reliability to award certificates following verification of conformance. It is advisable to check the accreditation status of such bodies prior to appointing them.

**Threat:** a potential cause of an unwanted incident, which may result in harm to a system or organisation.*

**UKAS:** United Kingdom Accreditation Service – the sole national accreditation body recognised by the UK government to assess, against internationally agreed standards, organisations that provide certification, testing, inspection and calibration services. See *www.ukas.com*.

**Vulnerability:** a weakness of an asset or control that can be exploited by one or more threats.* There are regularly updated central stores of known vulnerabilities at Bugtraq (*www.securityfocus.com/archive/1*), CVE (Common Vulnerabilities and Exposures – *http://cve.mitre.org/*) and in the SANS top 20 (SANS (SysAdmin, Audit, Network, Security) Institute – *www.sans.org/top20/*).

# ITG RESOURCES

IT Governance Ltd sources, creates and delivers products and services to meet the real-world, evolving IT governance needs of today's organisations, directors, managers and practitioners.

The ITG website (www.itgovernance.co.uk) is the international one-stop-shop for corporate and IT governance information, advice, guidance, books, tools, training and consultancy.

## Toolkits

ITG's unique range of toolkits includes the IT Governance Framework Toolkit, which contains all the tools and guidance that you will need in order to develop and implement an appropriate IT governance framework for your organisation.

There is also a wide range of toolkits to simplify implementation of management systems, such as an ISO/IEC 27001 ISMS, and these can all be viewed and purchased online at www.itgovernance.co.uk.

## Training Services

ISO/IEC 27001:2013 is the international management Standard that helps businesses and organisations throughout the world develop a best-in-class Information Security Management System. Knowledge and experience in implementing and maintaining ISO27001 compliance are considered to be essential to building a successful career in information security. We have the world's first programme of certificated ISO27001 education with Foundation, Lead Implementer, Risk Management and Lead Auditor training courses. Each course is designed to provide delegates with relevant knowledge and skills and an industry-recognised qualification awarded by the International Board for IT Governance Qualifications (IBITGQ).

Full details of all IT Governance training courses can be found at www.itgovernance.co.uk/training.aspx.

## Professional Services and Consultancy

At IT Governance, we understand that information, information security and information technology are always business issues, and not just IT ones. Our consultancy services assist you in managing information security strategies in harmony with business goals, conveying the right messages to your colleagues to support decision-making.

For more information about IT Governance Consultancy, see: www.itgovernance.co.uk/consulting.aspx.

## Publishing Services

IT Governance Publishing (ITGP) is the world's leading IT-GRC publishing imprint that is wholly owned by IT Governance Ltd. With books and tools covering all IT governance, risk and compliance frameworks, we are the publisher of choice for authors and distributors alike, producing unique and practical publications of the highest quality, in the latest formats available.

www.itgovernancepublishing.co.uk is the website dedicated to ITGP enabling both current and future authors, distributors, readers and other interested parties, to have easier access to more information. This allows ITGP website visitors to keep up to date with the latest publications and news.

## Newsletter

IT governance is one of the hottest topics in business today, not least because it is also the fastest moving.

You can stay up to date with the latest developments across the whole spectrum of IT governance subject matter, including; risk management, information security, ITIL and IT service management, project governance, compliance and so much more, by subscribing to ITG's core publications and topic alert emails.

Simply visit our subscription centre and select your preferences: www.itgovernance.co.uk/newsletter.aspx.

Lightning Source UK Ltd.
Milton Keynes UK
UKHW021902270220
359459UK00007B/185